5/04

MARIJUANA AND YOUR LUNGS
The Incredibly Disgusting Story

Debbie Stanley

the rosen publishing group's
rosen central
new york

Published in 2000 by The Rosen Publishing Group, Inc.
29 East 21st Street, New York, NY 10010

First Edition

Library of Congress Cataloging-in-Publication Data

Stanley, Debbie.
    Marijuana and your lungs : the incredibly disgusting story /
Debbie Stanley.
        p. cm.— (Incredibly disgusting drugs)
    Includes bibliographical references and index.
    Summary: Discusses marijuana, the most widely used illegal drug in the
United States, emphasizing its damaging physiological effects on the
mind and body, most especially the lungs.
    ISBN 0-8239-3252-4
    1. Marijuana abuse—Juvenile literature. 2. Marijuana—Toxicology—
Juvenile literature. [1. Marijuana. 2. Drug abuse.] I. Title. II. Series.

HV5822.M3 S83 2000
616.86'3507—dc21   00-025498

Manufactured in the United States of America

CONTENTS

Introduction: What Is Marijuana?

Marijuana is the most widely used illegal drug in the United States. Marijuana has lots of slang names, including pot, dope, reefer, ganja, grass, herb, Mary Jane, and weed. The cigarettes made from it are most often called joints. The part left over after a joint is smoked, like the butt of a cigarette, is called a roach. Police often bust users when they find roaches in their car ashtrays or in their houses. The process of smoking pot is known as getting high, or toking. Most people

roach

smoke dope, but sometimes they eat it. It is most commonly rolled into joints, but sometimes it is smoked in pipes or other devices. People who use marijuana are known as potheads, dopeheads, druggies, burnouts, stoners—or just losers.

WHERE IT COMES FROM

Marijuana is made from *Cannabis sativa,* or the hemp plant, which many users grow themselves. Hash and hash oil are also made from this plant. The leaf pattern of the plant is easy to recognize and is often used to illustrate CD covers, T-shirts, hats, and key chains. The police also find it easy to recognize when they see it growing in people's backyards and basements.

HOW IT WORKS

There is a chemical in marijuana called THC (tetrahydro-cannabinol), and that is what makes the user feel high. It also causes damage to the lungs and other parts of the body. THC stays in your body long after you have used pot, and it is what causes a drug test to come back positive. THC is also the reason that marijuana is classified as a psychotropic drug. This means that it has the power to change the way you experience the world around you; it distorts your perception of reality. It can make you feel good, or it can make you feel scared and panicky. You can't be sure that what you're seeing, hearing, or feeling is really there when you are high on marijuana.

POT IN OUR CULTURE

Pot became popular back in the 1960s, when people of the hippie counterculture brought it to the nation's attention. Hippies wore colorful clothes and jewelry, listened to rock music, and were in favor of peace. They protested against the Vietnam War, and many refused to go when they were drafted. They also did a lot of drugs, especially pot and LSD, which causes hallucinations. When you have

6

hallucinations, you see things that aren't actually there but seem totally real, like people-sized spiders or people's faces melting. Hippies believed that everyone should be kind to each other and help each other out, and many freely shared their drugs with others. This is how thousands of people got hooked on drugs during that time.

Drugs such as marijuana can cause hallucinations.

Many people thought hippies were dangerous because they encouraged young people to radically change their lives and rebel against society, but the thing that worried parents most was the drug use. Not much was known about the long-term effects of drug use at that time, but people have learned since then that all drugs, even the pot they swore was harmless, are actually addictive and damaging to the body and mind. Some drugs, especially LSD, can continue to affect people years after they last took them. People who used a lot of LSD back in the '60s have reported having flashbacks—scary episodes in which they hallucinate and act as if they have taken the drug again, when it has really been years since they last used it.

When marijuana became popular in the 1960s, it was much weaker than it is now. The amount of THC in it was much lower. But now THC is a lot more concentrated, making pot a much stronger and more dangerous drug than it was back then. Even worse, marijuana is often combined with other drugs to get a different effect or to make it cheaper to produce. If you buy pot from someone, you have no way of knowing what you are really getting. It is unlikely that it will be pure marijuana. It might have other drugs, such as PCP, mixed in that will cause different reactions and mess you up even more than pot alone. You could even end up overdosing on PCP and not even know it was in your joint.

8

IT KEEPS GETTING MORE DANGEROUS

Marijuana is the drug most likely to be described by users as safe. There is a lot of controversy over it. Fans of marijuana insist that it doesn't harm them and believe it should be made legal. If you do a search for "marijuana" on the Internet, you will find thousands of Web sites eager to tell you how safe and wonderful they

Sometimes pot is laced with other drugs, causing very bad reactions.

think pot really is. Some even include information on research that supposedly proves their point.

Studying this topic is a good way for you to learn not only about the dangers of marijuana but also about how research can be misused to "prove" either side of an

9

argument. It will also show you, if you don't know already, that there is a lot of false information on the Internet. It's a great tool, but it is not regulated or checked by anyone in authority, so anyone can build a Web page and say anything he or she wants, true or false. You have to be careful to check sources before you believe something you read on the Internet.

Be smart and look past all the hype—all those drug users trying to get you to join them—and see the very real dangers that come with drug use.

1 What It Does to Your Lungs

Your lungs convert the air you breathe into the oxygen and other gases your body needs to keep you alive. Those gases are transferred directly into your blood from your lungs. If you inhale smoke, the ingredients in that smoke are carried into your lungs and blood when you breathe. It's the same process whether you're breathing pure mountain air, city smog, or smoke from a house fire, cigarettes, or pot. Your lungs also remove "bad" air from your body. When you breathe out, you exhale carbon dioxide, a waste product your body needs to get rid of. This transfer of good air in and bad air out is made possible by the tiny, delicate air sacs inside your lungs, called alveoli. Alveoli are found at the end of the bronchial

MYTHS ABOUT POT

Don't knock it till you try it

Stoners will tell you it's not right for you to reject pot before you've tried it. A lot of kids fall for this line because their parents use the exact same method to get them to eat gross stuff like liver. Well, you knew your parents were tricking you with the food, so you should trust your instinct when it tells you that the pothead is fooling you, too. And the worst thing is, no one gets addicted to liver, but by trying pot, even just once, you could be on the road to becoming a drug addict.

There are lots of things in life that you don't have to try to know they are bad for you. Adults may seem dumb sometimes, but this is one case where learning from their experience can save you a lot of trouble.

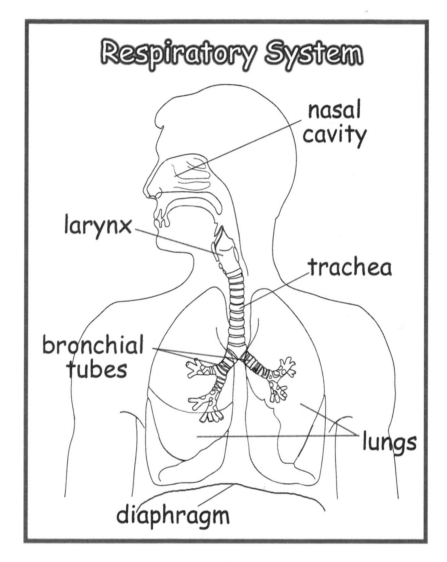

Respiratory System

- nasal cavity
- larynx
- trachea
- bronchial tubes
- lungs
- diaphragm

tubes. These air sacs are very soft and vulnerable, and in order to work correctly they have to stay clean, flexible, and healthy. They are meant to filter gases, not the tiny solid pieces that come in with polluted air, smoke, or air filled with pollen.

that residue just builds up in there, keeping the smoker's lungs from working right.

Breathing polluted air (including smoke) will, over time, give you all kinds of lung infections and diseases. One of the most important advances in our society was the invention of electricity. It reduced coal burning, which was dirty and unhealthy and caused millions of cases of asthma, emphysema, and lung cancer. The air you now breathe is much cleaner because people before you worked hard to save your lungs.

And yet some people don't appreciate how lucky they are to have clean air. They go ahead and make their own pollution by smoking cigarettes and pot.

DISEASE

By now everyone knows how unhealthy cigarette smoking is. We know that cigarettes put tar and nicotine into your body, coating your lungs with cancer-causing gunk and getting your brain addicted to smoking. Scientists have identified many cancer-causing ingredients in tobacco cigarettes, and many of those ingredients are also in marijuana. Even worse, many of those ingredients are stronger or more concentrated in pot than they are in cigarettes. And don't forget, marijuana also contains THC, which is an irritant to the lungs. On top of all that, people who smoke pot tend to inhale even more deeply than tobacco smokers do, and they actually hold their breath to keep the smoke in their lungs and get high faster. This allows all of those disease-causing ingredients to do even more damage in a shorter amount of time.

Here are some examples of lung diseases you might get if you smoke tobacco or marijuana, or if you are exposed to sec-ondhand smoke from someone smoking around you.

Asthma

Asthma is a potentially life-threatening condition that makes breathing difficult or impossible. A person who has an asthma attack can't get enough air into his or her lungs and may faint. Several things happen during an asthma attack: the bronchial tubes swell, the muscles around them squeeze tight, and mucus is trapped, causing the gasping feeling that is so frightening to asthma sufferers and those watching them struggle to breathe. Parents who smoke around their children may be giving them asthma. For people who have asthma, breathing any kind of smoke may trigger an attack.

Emphysema

As with asthma, emphysema makes you feel like you can't catch your breath. Your lungs become stiff, and the air sacs within them lose their ability to exchange the good air you breathe in with the carbon dioxide you breathe out. Your heart is forced to work much harder to compensate for the lack of oxygen coming in through your lungs.

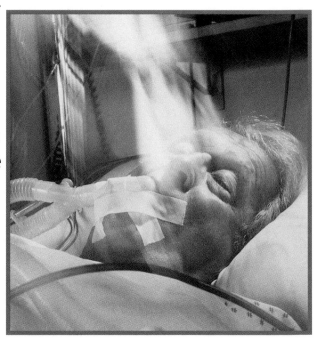

18

Eventually, your lungs or heart will just stop working and you will die trying to get enough air. But first, since emphysema develops slowly, you will most likely suffer years of pain, exhaustion, and being stuck with an oxygen tank and a wheelchair. Emphysema is incurable, and it is most often caused by smoking.

Lung Cancer

Lung cancer is almost always fatal. It usually spreads to other parts of the body before it is detected. Dying from lung cancer is extremely painful, and since it usually spreads, victims will have pain from other cancers at the same time. As their bodies slowly break down, their lungs become weak and begin to fill with fluid. They begin to make an eerie sound as they breathe, called a "death rattle." It sounds as if the victims have a bunch of sticky goop in their air passages, and they do.

Since it's so hard to breathe, lung cancer victims cough a lot. Every time they cough you would swear they are going to die from the effort. When they're not coughing, their breathing is very loud and strained and crackly sound-ing. If someone in your house has lung cancer, you will be able to hear their death-rattle breathing and their coughing throughout the entire house. In many cases, lung cancer

MYTHS ABOUT POT
It's not as bad for you as cigarettes

Saying that smoking marijuana isn't as bad as smoking cigarettes is NOT the same as saying that marijuana is good for you.

It is clearly not good for you. In fact, it may cause even more damage than cigarettes, because pot smokers hold the smoke in their lungs longer, and because pot, like cigarettes, contains potentially cancer-causing ingredients. Marijuana smoke damages your lungs just as any other smoke does. It also damages your brain cells. Smoking anything can give you lung cancer, which is usually fatal, or it can give you mouth or throat cancer, which might require a doctor to cut out your voice box or pieces of your mouth, lips, jaw, or tongue. They don't grow back.

victims actually die by drowning when fluids from inside their bodies seep into their lungs and fill them up.

Lung cancer is the most common cause of death from cancer for both men and women, and it is almost always caused by smoking or living with a smoker.

cancerous lung

healthy lung

Lung cancer is almost always fatal.

2 What It Does to Your Body

If asthma, emphysema, and lung cancer aren't enough to convince you that smoking cigarettes or pot is dangerous, there are dozens of other conditions and diseases for you to think about. Here are some of the other things that can go wrong with your body if you smoke.

HEART ATTACK

You're relaxing in your favorite chair when all of a sudden you feel like there is an elephant sitting on your chest. You can't breathe, you start to sweat, you have pain in your left arm, and the pain in your chest is worse than anything you have ever felt. You realize you're having a heart attack, and you start to panic because you know you might die and that you did it to yourself.

MYTHS ABOUT POT
They give it to cancer patients, so it must be okay

First of all, nobody gives marijuana to cancer patients—at least not legally. Doctors are not allowed to prescribe marijuana to patients.

Second, cancer patients are given drugs and treatments that can be damaging to the body but that help to kill cancer. Some patients are treated with dangerous radioactive material that causes painful side effects. So don't assume that everything a cancer patient uses for treatment is "healthy."

Third, cancer patients who use marijuana do so because their drug treatments make them nauseous and unable to eat. Some find that marijuana helps them to regain their appetite and tolerate pain. People dying of AIDS sometimes use marijuana, too. But sick people who use pot are still breaking the law. The people who get the marijuana for them—usually family members—could also be arrested for "dealing" and could spend a long time in jail.

You have been smoking pot and cigarettes since you were in high school. Now you—and your innocent family members—are going to pay.

Smoking causes heart disease when the heart muscle itself becomes weak and doesn't work right. Smoking also leads to hardening of the arteries, or arteriosclerosis, when fatty deposits start to stick to the insides of blood vessels instead of being swept away in the bloodstream. Over time, the arteries become stiff and hard, rough on the inside instead of smooth, and they start to close up. An artery that is as big around as a garden hose can end up with an opening inside that is barely as big as a tooth-pick. Either heart

Smoking causes atheroma, or fatty deposits in the arteries. This in turn causes arteriosclerosis, which can lead to heart attack and stroke.

disease or hardening of the arteries is, by itself, enough to cause a heart attack. In smokers, they often occur together in the same person, making that person's risk of heart attack much higher.

STROKE

You are walking through the kitchen and you reach to open the fridge—but your arm won't move. You try to call out for someone to help you—but you can't speak. The next thing you know, you are in a hospital bed, and your family is standing around you, crying, and you can't say anything. Everything on one side of your body is dead and won't move. You've had a stroke, and now all you can do is watch your loved ones suffering and wish you hadn't smoked.

Smoking causes high blood pressure, which can lead to a stroke. Hardening of the arteries, which can cause a heart attack, can also cause a stroke. A stroke is like a heart attack, but it takes place in your brain—it's a "brain attack." A stroke deprives your brain of blood, and brains don't last very long without blood. If you get to a hospital fast, you might be left with only a few side effects, like not being able to walk or talk. But a lot of people don't get there fast enough, or the stroke is too big to fix, and they die.

AMPUTATION

For a while now, your feet have felt cold. No matter how many pairs of socks you put on, no matter how much time you spend under the electric blanket, they never warm up, and they don't have any feeling in them. You think that maybe it is your imagination, but they are starting to look kind of bluish green. You go to the doctor expecting to come home with a prescription, but instead you get put in the hospital. You do finally come home a week later—without your feet!

Smoking decreases blood circulation, especially to the extremities—your hands and feet—which are farthest from your heart. Over time, your circulation can become so weak that those extremities actually die from lack of blood. If they aren't amputated—cut off by a surgeon—they will rot and spread infection through your entire body, killing you.

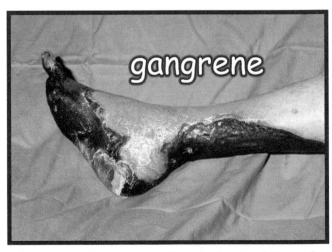

gangrene

Gangrene is the death of the body's soft tissue caused by a loss of blood supply. It causes such extreme decay that amputation is the only remedy.

CANCER FROM HEAD TO TOE

You notice a strange spot on your tongue, but since it doesn't hurt, you ignore it until your next doctor's visit. You show the spot to the doctor, who sends you to a cancer specialist. The cancer doctor does some tests, and you find out that the pain-less little spot is cancer. The cancer doctor schedules you for surgery, and after the procedure he comes in and tells you how lucky you are because they got all the cancer before it spread to other parts of your body. He says that people who smoke, like you, get not only tongue cancer, like you did, but also cancers of the throat, voice box, bladder, kidneys, pancreas, liver, heart, bones, brain, and, especially, the lungs. He tells you again how lucky you are, and you would like to thank him, but you can't speak: In order to save your life, the doctor had to cut out your tongue.

cancer

Removal of this cancerous tumor in the mouth will probably leave this person with a permanent speech impairment or disfigurement. Such cancerous lesions are the result of persistent smoking over many years.

Cancer-causing ingredients, or carcinogens, are found in smoke from both tobacco and marijuana. When you inhale, these carcinogens get into your blood and are carried to every part of your body. They look for the weakest spots and attack them, causing cancer to grow. There is no way to predict where you will get cancer first, but it's a pretty good bet that sooner or later you will have it somewhere.

ACCIDENTS

You are floating above the scene, looking down on the nastiest mess you have ever seen. Somebody is sprawled across a bed, and there is a huge red splatter on the wall behind him. He looks like a kid about your age, in jeans and a T-shirt. You look more closely to see if you know him, but half the kid's face is gone. You start to remember something . . . you and a couple friends smoked a little weed and started daring each other to do stuff. One kid remembered your mom carries a little gun in her purse and dared you to go get it. You got the gun, took another hit off the joint, and laughed as you put the gun to your head, saying, "Duh, this is your brain on drugs!" And now you're looking down at this kid with half a head, in this room that looks like your room, in clothes that look like your clothes.

Tobacco and marijuana have a lot of the same physical dangers, but marijuana use has an additional risk: accidents. Since smoking pot makes you clumsy and uncoordinated, makes you react more slowly, and makes you more likely to take risks, the chances of getting hurt in some sort of accident go way up when you're high. You might do something really stupid that you would normally never do, like playing with a gun or jumping off the garage or breaking into the school to set the science lab on fire. If you are old enough to drive or have friends who are, you might think you can drive fine—maybe even better—when you're stoned, but you'll find out how wrong you are when you blow through a red light and get T-boned by a truck coming the other way.

Being stoned might cause you to take dangerous—and sometimes deadly—risks.

MYTHS ABOUT POT
It will relax you

So will being knocked unconscious by a base-ball bat to the head. Such a blow will make your muscles relax, slow your heart rate, and make you temporarily unaware of your problems. But you may never be normal again. All of this is true of pot, too.

There are hundreds of better ways to relax, including meditation, deep breathing, talking to friends, reading, and exercise. You are much better off trying those first. You wouldn't risk having someone knock you out just so you could relax, so don't do it to yourself with marijuana.

3 What It Does to Your Mind

Okay. Assuming that you are lucky enough to escape physical injury or death, what kind of life do you think you will have as a pothead? Probably not the one you could have had.

POT LIMITS YOUR POTENTIAL

There is no way to scientifically prove that people who smoke pot could have been smarter or accomplished more in their lives if they had stayed away from drugs. But there are a lot of people who have smoked pot all their lives and have looked back and realized that they could have gone to college or had a better career or a happier family life, but they never seemed to

MYTHS ABOUT POT
It will make you creative

What this means is that you will be able to write great poetry, songs, or stories, or paint beautiful pictures, or play a musical instrument more skillfully. The truth is that you may THINK you are doing all of these things better, but this is a load of bull. You don't need to do drugs to be a better poet, artist, or musician. What you do need is practice and dedication. Drugs only get in the way of that.

There is one way that doing pot will make you creative, however. Drug users become very creative at lying, stealing, and making excuses. They spend a lot of time and mental energy (what little there is left after all that drug use) coming up with stories for their parents, teachers, bosses, and the police. Eventually, almost every drug user gets caught and has to face the consequences. There aren't a whole lot of outlets for creativity once you've been kicked out of school, fired from work, or locked up in jail.

get around to it. When you do drugs, you never seem to get around to a lot of things.

There is research that shows that people who regularly use pot end up with memory and coordination problems, even after they stop using the drug. They may have constant fatigue and apathy. You don't have to be a rocket scientist to figure out that if pot smoking makes people slower and weaker and less energized, users are not going to reach their full potential. And from that you should be able to see that pot will limit your opportunities, too.

POT STEALS YOUR SELF-ESTEEM

People develop drug habits to make up for something that is missing from their lives. In a lot of cases, that missing thing is self-esteem. They don't feel good about themselves, and they are uncomfortable around other people. Most people doubt themselves and struggle with low self-esteem at some point in their lives, but they develop methods for coping and then grow into stronger people.

Some people skip that growth process and turn to drugs for artificial confidence. They think they are more fun to be around, and they don't feel like such losers when they

Pot smoking can keep you from living up to your full potential.

are high. They get addicted to the way drugs make them feel, and by constantly doing drugs, they never learn how to feel good about themselves without getting high first. They never learn how to deal with the awkwardness and discomfort of getting along with other people, or the pain that comes from sad things like the death of a family member, or everyday disappointments like bad grades or not being picked for a team or a play. Sadly, they also cheat themselves out of enjoying the good things in life, like reaching a goal or being praised by a parent. Drugs dull ALL your feelings, good or bad.

POT MAKES YOU AN ESCAPE ARTIST

Constantly blunting your pain with drugs will leave you unable to cope with reality. Using pot to escape from problems and disappointments means you will never become a mature person who is worthy of respect from others. No one will ever come to you for advice. No one will ever trust you to be in charge of anything. Emotionally, you will never become a complete person. Your biggest achievement won't come from living your life, but from escaping from it.

4 Why Else Is It Bad for Me?

If you have already read chapters 1 through 3, it should be obvious that marijuana can do serious damage to your body and mind. But if that's not enough to convince you not to smoke pot, here are some other dangers to think about.

NOBODY WANTS A DRUGGIE

If you smoke pot or do any other illegal drugs, you will have a hard time getting a job. And it's not just the fancy, high-paying jobs that do drug testing now—fast-food restaurants, car washes, and grocery stores do it, too. Employers don't want to hire people who are going to blow off work because they are stoned, or steal from the cash register to get drug money, or come to work high and have accidents that will cost the company money.

Sports teams test for drugs, too. Athletes aren't allowed to use any drugs, such as steroids, that will make them perform better than other players, and they're not allowed to use any illegal drugs like pot. So if you want to be on any kind of team, you have to stay off drugs.

And before you start thinking you can smoke pot and get it out of your system before you have to take a drug test, think again. Drug testing is getting much more sophisticated and harder to beat. The THC in pot is absorbed mostly in fatty tissues and can be detected in urine tests a month or more after you use it. So you might think you can just stay away from pot for the month before you know you'll be tested. But get this: Many drug-testing companies are now using hair samples because drugs never

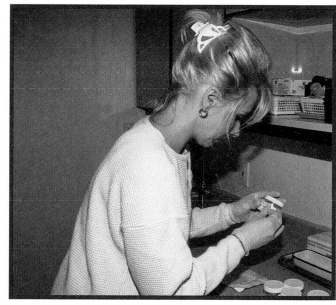

Many companies now test employees for drug use.

MYTHS ABOUT POT

It's fun

What is fun about sucking noxious smoke into your lungs, coughing and gagging on it, and then doing things you wouldn't normally do, like eating too much or drinking alcohol or having sex, all because marijuana impaired your judgment? What is fun about trying to do normal things, like riding your bike, or crossing a street, or speaking clearly to your parents, and finding out that you can't? What is fun about being out of control like that?

And remember, drugs cost a lot of money. What is so fun about being broke AND out of control?

come out of your hair. It's not just ON your hair—it's actually IN it. Since your hair grows only about half an inch per month, hair analysis can nail you for drugs you used more than a year ago.

You don't even have to smoke pot yourself for it to show up in your system. If you are around when other people are smoking it, you breathe in their secondhand smoke and your body absorbs it. There's even a new test that can detect microscopic amounts on your hands. So even if you don't actually do pot, you'll still be penalized for hanging out with people who do.

And speaking of your friends, you might have noticed that the people who do drugs stick together and don't mix very much with the people who don't. You have to decide: Are you going to be a burnout, or are you going to be drug-free? That decision will also decide for you who your friends will be. Do you want to hang out with people who want to make something of their lives, or do you want to be with the ones who will end up in jail, or in the hospital with some horrible disease, or, at best, working at a minimum-wage job? And before you start thinking you can do both—be friends with drug-free people and with druggies—you better realize that when you are with a group of people who think drugs are great, they will keep telling you how great drugs are and it will be really hard for you to resist joining in. You will never be able to convince them that drugs are bad. If you try, they will eventually dump you. And if you don't do drugs with them, they will eventually dump you. So if you're not in it to do drugs, why are you with them?

YOU'LL GET LOTS OF ATTENTION FROM COPS

Many pot users are so open about it, they seem to forget that smoking pot is illegal. You can definitely get arrested for using pot, and you can definitely do time in a juvenile facility or in jail for having it, especially if the authorities think you planned on giving it to others. If the police catch you with enough pot on you to share with others, or if they find you growing it yourself, you can be prosecuted as a dealer and be put away for a long time. One girl who had no previous record was arrested after she sent her boyfriend some drugs—he got only three years in jail, but she received the mandatory minimum of TEN YEARS. She'll spend ten years in jail for sending her boyfriend a present just once!

Just because pot is considered less dangerous than drugs like heroin and cocaine, don't think the cops will cut

MYTHS ABOUT POT

Everybody does it

Not true. The fact is, most people don't do ANY illegal drugs. But even if they did, why would you follow them? Smart people know that they don't have to do what everyone else is doing. Instead, they figure out for themselves what they think is right and do that, whether others do or not. Smart people also think before they act, and they stay away from people who act recklessly: That keeps them from doing stupid things like drugs.

you any slack. They know something about pot that keeps them interested in pot-heads: Marijuana is considered a "gateway" drug, meaning that for many people it opens the gate to using other drugs and committing crimes to get money for drugs. You might think that you have the self-control to use pot and not use anything heavier, but you have to remember that pot changes the way you think. It may turn you into a different person—one who will do bad things to keep getting high.

Another thing that is illegal if you are underage—smoking cigarettes—can also lead to smoking pot. Once you've caved in to pressure from tobacco company advertising and other kids and started smoking cigarettes, the chances that you will try pot are higher. So cigarettes are actually a gateway to pot, and pot is a gateway to other drugs and to crime.

YOU'LL BE A BABY ALL YOUR LIFE

This is probably the saddest thing of all about people who are regular pot users: They never grow up. The drug sucks the potential out of them and they settle for a life that is less than what they could have had if they had stayed away from drugs. They never learn how to handle life's problems with maturity and wisdom. They just keep hiding behind a high. No one respects them because they haven't earned respect. They haven't struggled to become successful or to get past the random obstacles life has thrown at them—like a screwed-up childhood, or a learning disability, or a physical handicap. Instead, they turned to drugs to bury their pain. The pain is still there, and it always will be until they stop doing drugs and face it. But by that point, they may have already done damage to their bodies that can't be repaired. They will still be better off without the drugs, but they might never be as smart or as strong as they could have been if they had never started smoking pot.

GLOSSARY

acquired immune deficiency syndrome (AIDS) An incurable disease that can cause severe pain and nausea; some AIDS patients use marijuana to enable them to eat.

arteriosclerosis Also known as hardening of the arteries; a condition in which the blood vessels become clogged with fatty deposits, often leading to a heart attack or stroke.

asthma A condition in which the bronchial tubes swell or close up, making breathing difficult or impossible.

carcinogens Cancer-causing substances, such as those found in cigarettes and marijuana.

chemotherapy Treatment for cancer that can cause severe nausea and inability to eat; some patients use marijuana to help them tolerate these side effects.

tetrahydrocannabinol (THC) The chemical in marijuana that causes the "high" and that is detected in drug tests.

FOR MORE INFORMATION

In the United States

Alliance for Cannabis Therapeutics
Web site: http://www.marijuana-as-
    medicine.org/alliance.htm

American Cancer Society
(800) ACS-2345
Web site: http://www.cancer.org

American Heart Association
7272 Greenville Avenue
Dallas, TX 75231
(800) AHA-USA1
Web site: http://www.american
    heart.org

Food and Drug Administration
HFI-40
Rockville, MD 20857
(888) INFO-FDA (463-6332)
Web site: http://www.fda.gov
e-mail: webmail@oc.fda.gov

National Center for
    Tobacco-Free Kids
(800) 284-KIDS
Web site: http://www.tobacco
    freekids.org
e-mail: info@tobaccofreekids.org

Partnership for a Drug-Free America
405 Lexington Avenue
16th Floor
New York, NY 10174
Web site: http://www.drugfree
    america.org

In Canada

Internet Mental Health
Suite 902—601 West Broadway
Vancouver, BC V5Z 4C2
(604) 876-2254
Web site: http://www.mental
    health.com

FOR FURTHER READING

Baum, Joanne, and Nancy Nielson. *The Truth About Pot: Ten Marijuana Users Share Their Personal Stories.* Edina, MN: Johnson Institute, 1996.

Glass, George. *Drugs and Fitting In.* New York: Rosen Publishing Group, 1998.

Hasday, Judy L., and Therese De Angelis. *Marijuana.* Philadelphia, PA: Chelsea House, 1999.

Konieczko, Craig. *Intervention.* New York: The Rosen Publishing Group, 2000.

Schleichert, Elizabeth. *Marijuana.* Minneapolis, MN: Enslow, 1996.

Somdahl, Gary L. *Marijuana Drug Dangers.* Minneapolis, MN: Enslow, 1999.

INDEX

CREDITS

About the Author

Debbie Stanley has a bachelor's degree in journalism and a master's degree in industrial and organizational psychology.

Photo Credits

Photo on pp. 4 and 42 John Bentham; pp. 5, 26 © Custom Medical Stock Photo ; p. 7 Bill Brady; p. 9 by Sarah Friedman; p. 14 © Gary Carlson/Photo Researchers; p. 17 K. Artz; p. 18 © Ken Tannenbaum/International Stock; p. 21 © A. Glauberman/Photo Researchers; p. 24 © Biophoto Associates/Photo Researchers; p. 27 © Biophoto Associates/Photo Researchers; p. 29 © Corbis; p. 34 by Shalhevet Moshe; p. 37 Ira Fox.

Series Design

Laura Murawski

Layout

Law Alsobrook